Shadrick K. Hooper, Denver and Rio Grande Railroad
Company

Rhymes of the Rockies

What the Poets Have Found to Say of the Beautiful Scenery on the Denver

and Rio Grande Railroad

Shadrick K. Hooper, Denver and Rio Grande Railroad Company

Rhymes of the Rockies
What the Poets Have Found to Say of the Beautiful Scenery on the Denver and Rio Grande Railroad

ISBN/EAN: 9783744726719

Printed in Europe, USA, Canada, Australia, Japan

Cover: Foto ©Thomas Meinert / pixelio.de

More available books at **www.hansebooks.com**

RHYMES OF THE ROCKIES:

OR,

WHAT THE POETS HAVE FOUND TO SAY

OF THE

BEAUTIFUL SCENERY

ON THE

DENVER & RIO GRANDE RAILROAD,

THE SCENIC LINE OF THE WORLD.

EIGHTH EDITION, 200,000

CHICAGO:
POOLE BROS., PRINTERS AND ENGRAVERS.
1891.

PRESENTATION.

This little Book of Poems,

Descriptive of Scenes among the Rocky Mountains

as viewed from trains
of
The Denver & Rio Grande Railroad,

is presented with the

compliments

of

S. K. Hooper

General Passenger Agent.

COPIES OF "RHYMES OF THE ROCKIES" WILL BE SENT TO ANY ADDRESS ON APPLICATION TO

S. K. Hooper, General Passenger Agent, · · · Denver.
F. A. Wadleigh, Ass't Gen'l Pass'r and Ticket Agent, Denver.
W. B. Cobb, General Eastern Agent, 379 Broadway, New York.
J. W. Slosson, General Agent, 236 Clark St., · · Chicago.
L. B. Eveland, Traveling Agent, 105 W. 9th St., Kansas City.
W. F. Tibbits, Traveling Agent, · · · · Denver.
A. N. Oliver, City Passenger Agent, · · · Denver.
W. M. Rank, General Agent, 204 Front St., · San Francisco.

PREFACE.

WHEREVER Nature appears in her grander moods, her inspiration stirs the heart and the imagination, and whether it be the "Banks and Braes o' Bonnie Doon," the Crags of the "Rio de Las Animas," "The Royal Gorge," the rocky declivities of "Ben Venue" or the cleft summit of "The Mount of the Holy Cross," the poetic spirit is invoked and a rhythmic offering laid upon the altar of the muses. The picturesque countries of the old world have been immortalized in song, and to show that Colorado, one of the newest portions of the new world, has not failed to inspire the same sentiments in the hearts of none the less sincere poets, this book has been prepared. Upon these pages are presented a few of the contributions to poetic literature incited by beholding scenes grander and more varied than those of Scotland, Italy or Switzerland, all the more valuable because spontaneous and therefore expressive of genuine emotions. In order that nothing may be lacking in the conveying of a vivid impression, pictures which are works of art supplement the poems, and to further assist the imagination of those who have not beheld these scenes and to refresh the memory of those who have beheld them, brief but accurate descriptions have been added. In a work of this character, brevity must be observed and only typical poems and scenes have been selected. The mid-continent region traversed by the Denver & Rio Grande Railroad possesses without doubt the most magnificent scenery in the world and the difficulty has been, not what to select, but what to omit. As it is, this book must be considered as only a hint as to what exists in the wonderland of the Rocky mountains and its object will be attained if it excite an intelligent interest in the most picturesque portion of our country.

PRELUDE.

My country 'tis of thee,
Sweet land of liberty,
 Of thee I sing;
Land where our fathers died,
Land of the pilgrim's pride,
From every mountain side
 Let Freedom ring.

My native country, thee,
Land of the noble free—
 Thy name I love;
I love thy rocks and rills,
Thy woods and templed hills;
My heart with rapture thrills
 Like that above.

Let music swell the breeze,
And ring from all the trees,
 Sweet freedom's song;
Let mortal tongues awake,
Let all that breathe partake,
Let rocks their silence break,
 The sound prolong.

Our father's God to thee,
Author of Liberty,
 To thee I sing;
Long may our land be bright
With freedom's holy light;
Protect us by thy might,
 Great God, our King.

PALMER LAKE

PALMER LAKE.

PALMER LAKE, in addition to being a place of
exceeding beauty, is a natural curiosity, poised, as
it is, exactly on the summit of the "Divide," a spur
of the outlying range of the Rockies, extending eastward
into the great plains, and from this summit the waters of
the lake flow northward to the Platte and southward to
the Arkansas. Approached from either Denver or Pueblo,
via the Denver & Rio Grande Railroad, it breaks suddenly
upon the sight, a vision of sylvan beauty and delight.
Red-roofed, picturesque cottages nestle here and there
among the hills, gaily-painted boats float gracefully upon
the bright blue waters, a fountain in the center flings its
spray half a hundred feet into the air, and on either hand
rugged peaks, pine-clad and broken by castellated rocks,
rise into a sky whose cerulean hue is reflected by the
placid waters of the lake. Excellent hotels and livery
establishments furnish good accommodations for sojourn-
ers. Surely here can be found the realization of Petrarch's
lines:

.   .   .   " The ray
Of a bright sun can make sufficient holiday,
Developing the mountains, leaves and flowers,
And shining in the brawling brook, whereby,
Clear as its current, glide the sauntering hours
With a calm languor, which, though to the eye
Idlesse it seem, hath its morality."

Closely contiguous is Glen Park, an assembly ground
modeled after the famous Chautauqua and destined to
become equally as popular in the West as its prototype in
the East. Objects of natural interest are abundant and
the walks and drives to Glen D'Eau, Bellview Point, Ben
Lomond, the Arched Rocks and the cañons and glens
adjacent afford material for enjoyment in the seeing and
for many pleasant memories.

PALMER LAKE.

W. E. PABOR.

Serene and sweet and smiling as a bride
Nestles Lake Palmer on the green Divide;
The hills around it, the blue sky above,
The summer sunshine bathing it in love;
Fair as the lochs that lie in Scotia's glens,
Worthy the praise that comes from poets' pens.
Its sparkling waters in the sunshine gleam
Full of the glamour of the sweetest dream.

Toward the sunset, in the green defile,
The pine trees rustle and the wild flowers smile;
The crystal waters of the creek flow by,
White as the snows that on the mountains lie;
Within the shadow bits of sunshine rest
Like diamonds gleaming from an umber nest;
Wild roses blush at kisses given by bees
And black-birds twitter underneath the trees.

The waters ripple to the lake's green shore,
Timing the dipping of the boatman's oar;
The fountain glistens in the sun's warm beams,
The white spray falling down in rainbow streams;
The air is full of melody and sound,
Voices float out as if from fairy ground,
And all our thoughts to happy fancies run
Under the languor of the summer sun.

Oh! lake of beauty, glen of sweet content!
On the headwaters of the Monument;
The hills that hide thee, and each bosky dell
That nestles near thee, but one story tell;
To those who love fair Nature when she waits
And smiles a welcome at the open gates,
Where Pleasure stands to lead to leaf-robed nooks
And sweet delights we cannot find in books.

GATEWAY TO THE GARDEN OF THE GODS.

THE GARDEN OF THE GODS.

THE GARDEN OF THE GODS is a valley of wonders easily accessible from Manitou. Approached from the west the entrance is through what may aptly be called a postern gate in contrast with the entrance from the east through the grand gateway. In this solitude nature has perpetrated many strange freaks of sculpture and of architecture, as if she were diverting herself after the strain of the mighty mood in which the mountains were brought forth. Solitude is here unbroken by the residence of man, but inanimate forms of stone supply quaint and grotesque suggestions of life. Here are found hints of Athens and the Parthenon, Palmyra and the Pyramids, Karnac and her crumbling columns. Many of these monoliths are nearly tabular and reach the height of three and four hundred feet. Two of the loftier ones, with a small space between, make the two portals of the famed gateway. After their form, their most striking feature is their color, which glows with an intensity of red unknown in any of the sandstones of the east. Standing outlined against a spotless sky of blue, with the white light of the sun falling upon them, these portals flash with the bright splendor of carnelian. The inanimate forms have received appropriate designations. There is a "Statue of Liberty," a "Cathedral Spire," a "Dolphin," a "Bear and Seal," a "Lion," a "Griffin," and hundreds of other quaint and curious figures, making a list far too extended for recapitulation here. No words can describe the weird attractions of this wonderful garden, which, once beheld, however, can never be forgotten. The impression is of something mighty, unreal and supernatural. Of the gods surely—but of the gods of the Norse Walhalla in some of their strange outbursts of wild rage or uncouth playfulness.

THE GARDEN OF THE GODS.

WILLIAM ALLEN BUTLER.

Beneath the rocky peak that hides
  In clouds its snow-flecked crest,
Within these crimson crags abides
  An Orient in the West.
These tints of flame, these myriad dyes,
  This Eastern desert calm,
Should catch the gleam of Syrian skies,
  Or shade of Egypt's palm.

As if to bar the dawn's first light
  These ruby gates are hung;
As if from Sinai's frowning height
  These riven tablets flung.
But not the Orient's drowsy gaze,
  Young Empire's opening lids
Greet these strange shapes, of earlier days
  Than Sphinx or Pyramids.

Here the New West its wealth unlocks,
  And tears the veil aside,
Which hides the mystic glades and rocks
  The Red man deified.
This greensward, girt with tongues of flame,
  With spectral pillars strewn,
Not strangely did the savage name
  A haunt of gods unknown.

Hard by the gentle Manitou
  His healing fountains poured;
Blood-red, against the cloudless blue,
  These storm-tossed Titans soared.

      *   *   *   *   *   *

With torrents wild and tempest blast,
  And fierce volcanic fires,
In secret moulds has Nature cast
  Her monoliths and spires.

Their shadows linger where we tread,
  Their beauty fills the place;
A broken shrine—its votaries fled—
  A spurned and vanished race.
Untouched by Time the garden gleams,
  Unplucked the wild flower shines,
And the scarred summit's rifted seams
  Are bright with glistening pines.

And still the guileless heart that waits
  At Nature's feet may find,
Within the rosy, sun-lit gates,
  A hidden glory shrined.
His presence feel to whom, in fear,
  Untaught, the savage prayed,
And, listening in the garden, hear
  His voice, nor be afraid.

MANITOU SPRINGS AND PIKES PEAK.

MANITOU.

MANITOU is the ideal summer resort, having been favored by nature with healing springs equal, if not superior, in efficacy to those of Ems or Spa or Saratoga, and being surrounded by scenery more beautiful, grand and varied than that of any similar resort in the world. Here is an Arcadian valley, lying at the foot of Pike's Peak, protected by encircling mountains and enlivened by the foam-bedecked, flashing waters of the Fountain que Bouille, which, full of the sprightliness of its youth in Ute Pass and its escapade at Rainbow Falls, comes dashing and splashing and singing its happy song:

> " I chatter over stony ways,
>   In little sharps and trebles:
> I hubble into eddying bays,
>   I babble on the pebbles."

This valley is made the site of a village, picturesque in its construction and abounding in hotels which rival in elegance and luxury those of the famous Eastern watering-places. With a climate renowned for its salubrity, with medicinal springs of acknowledged superiority, with pure air, bright sunshine and a walk or drive leading to some new object of interest for each day in the week, Manitou has justly received the palm as the most charming of summer resorts. Easily accessible, being a station on the Denver & Rio Grande Railroad, only three hours' ride from Denver or Pueblo, it is thronged each season by the wealth, cultivation and fashion, not only of Colorado, but also of the East, from all parts of which may be found representatives whose days of enjoyment here not only secure their return, but also the presence of their friends, attracted by the glowing reports of those who have experienced its manifold attractions.

MANITOU.

EDGAR P. VANGASSEN.

Where the shadow of the mountain
Meets the sunshine of the fountain,
Listen to these voices singing
And the message they are bringing :

SPIRIT OF THE SPRINGS:

Sister spirit of the stream
Is it real or a dream?
Faces in their color change,
Voices take a wider range;
Nature's emerald bosom shows
Charm and color of the rose;
Tell me, spirit, is it true,
All things old give place to new?

SPIRIT OF THE SPRINGS:

Sister spirit of the stream
It is real, not a dream!
Echoes as from Eden wake
Music such as seraphs make
In each glen and through each rift
Where your shining waters drift;
While the song of youth and maid
. Crown each cool and shadowed glade.

SPIRIT OF THE STREAM:

Sister spirit of the spring,
Fresher, clearer voices sing
Of a whiter, later race
Taking the swart Indian's place.
Art to Nature gives her hand;
Fashion waves her magic wand,
And the languorous glamour cast
Veils the glory of the past.

SPIRIT OF THE STREAM:

From the peak down which I flow
With my water born of snow,
To the valley lands that lie
'Neath a warm and sunny sky,
All the air is full of change,
Change as sweet as it is strange;
And my song forever chimes .
To these later, happier times.

THE SPIRITS OF THE SPRINGS AND STREAM:

Whiter tepees crown our hills,
Sweeter lips now touch our rills;
Under Manitou's bright skies
Fairer faces meet our eyes;
And where crystal waters glide
Happy lovers blush and hide;
Dusky features fade away,
Saxon faces crown To-Day.

Flash on fountain, roll on river,
Snow-crowned peak and sun-kissed vale;
These are Nature's gifts forever,
Until Nature's self shall fail.

IN CHEYENNE CAÑON.

CHEYENNE CAÑON.

CHEYENNE CAÑON is full of surprises. A pleasant drive of four miles from Colorado Springs brings one to the place. The vulgar linear measure of its length is out of harmony with the winding path, over rocks, between straight pines and across the rushing waters of the brook that boils down the whole rocky cut. The narrow gorge ends in a round well of granite, down one side of which leaps, slides, foams and rushes a series of cascades—seven falls in line pouring the water from the melted snow above into this cup. In this deep hollow only the noonday sun ever shines. Going up the cañon, with the roar of the waters ahead and the winding path before one, the loftiness and savage wildness of the walls catch only a dizzying glance, but coming out their sides seem to touch the heavens and to be measureless. The eye can hardly take in the vast height and, with the after-noon sun touching only the extreme tops, one realizes in what a crevice and fissure of the rocks the cañon winds. A comparison between this and the Via Mala and the other wild gorges of the Alps is impossible, but had legend and history and poetry followed it for centuries Cheyenne cañon would have its great features acknowledged. Above the waterfall, on the eastward slope of Cheyenne mountain, is the grave of one of America's truest poets and most remarkable women, "H. H." . Here the late Helen Hunt Jackson lies asleep among the scenes she loved.

> "Such graves as these are pilgrims' shrines—
> Shrines to no codes or creed confined,
> The Delphian Vales, the Palestines,
> The Meccas of the mind."

Cheyenne cañon has henceforth and forever a profounder meaning, its unexampled beauty being supplemented by a sacred and tender memory.

CHEYENNE CAÑON.

STANLEY WOOD.

Oh, Cheyenne cañon! in thy dim defiles,
Where glooms the light, as through cathedral aisles,
Where flash and fall bright waters, pure as air,
Where wild birds brood, wild blossoms bloom, and where
The wind sings anthems through the darkling trees,
A presence breathes the tenderest melodies,

Songs that the finer ears of poets feel
But do not hear, ethereal chords that steal
Upon the soul, as fragrance of the flowers,
Unseen, unknown, from undiscovered bowers,
Enwraps the senses with a deep delight,
Pure as the stars and tender as the night.

For here in Nature's arms there lies asleep
One who loved Nature with a passion deep,
Who knew her language and who read her book,
Who sang her music, which the bird, the brook,
The winds, the woods, the mountains and the seas
Chant ever, in commingling harmonies.

Oh, Cheyenne cañon! through thy dim defiles
The music floats as through cathedral aisles;
The singer silent, but the song is heard
In sigh of wind and carolling of bird.
All these the poet's melodies prolong,
For Nature now sings o'er her loved one's song.

VETA PASS AND DUMP MOUNTAIN.

VETA PASS.

FROM VETA PASS one beholds a scene of great magnificence, but it is not alone the view that repays the tourist; the ascent itself is fraught with the profoundest interest. The Denver & Rio Grande Railroad accomplishes the summit by a series of stupendous grades and the most remarkable curve in the history of railroad engineering. The "muleshoe curve" is a scientific achievement worth a trip across the continent to see. The road is a mere groove cut in the side of the mountain, which is so steep that a boulder set in motion goes thundering down and does not stop until it reaches the bottom of the gorge. But thrilling as this passage is, up the sinuous roadway along the mountain side, it has no real elements of danger in it. No accident has ever happened here and, should a part of the train break away, it would be stopped in less than a car's length by the prompt action of the automatic brake with which all trains on this mountain-climbing system are provided. But it is from the summit of the Pass that one looks upon a scene of stupendous magnificence. From the pinnacle he gazes eastward to the dim horizon line where the cloudless sky shuts down upon the ever-widening plains, broken, to the south, by the symmetrical Spanish peaks. Turning to the west, he sees the majestic form of Sierra Blanca, the loftiest mountain in the Rocky range, and rendered more remarkable by its triple peak, while, to the north, La Veta mountain stands stupendous and sublime. The climb has been difficult up the tremendous grade of 211 feet to the mile, but, when the apex has been reached, the train glides into the timber and halts at the handsome stone station over nine thousand feet above the level of the distant sea.

VETA PASS.

EDGAR PEARSON.

Imperial heights of Veta's star-crowned crest!
　　Entranced with rapture on the Pass I stand,
San Luis park, an empire, to the west,
　　Sky-piercing peaks upreared on every hand.

Chiefest of all Sierra Blanca towers,
　　Monarch of mountains, whose imperial frown
Marks him supreme among these giant powers,
　　Whose Titan brow upbears a triple crown.

Serenely grand against the azure sky,
　　Far to the east, the Spanish peaks uprear
Twin pyramids, snow-crowned and high,
　　A dream of Egypt to the sight appear.

A granite ocean slumbers at my feet,
　　Whose waves are mountains and whose foam is snow;
The clouds beneath me, like a ghostly fleet,
　　Sail slowly by, but whither none may know.

Below the serpent path, the sinuous coil,
　　By which we pass beyond these granite bars,
Bears witness that it is alone by toil
　　Mankind may reach at last the shining stars.

SIERRA BLANCA—THE HIGHEST MOUNTAIN IN COLORADO.

SIERRA BLANCA.

SIERRA BLANCA is the monarch of the Rocky range and the loftiest mountain, with one exception, in the United States. It is characterized by the peculiarity of a triple peak and rises directly from the plain to the stupendous height of 14,469 feet, over two miles and three-fifths of sheer ascent. A magnificent view of this mountain is obtained from the cars of the Denver & Rio Grande Railroad as soon as the descent from Veta Pass into the San Luis Valley has been made. Surely it is worth a journey across the continent to obtain a view of such a mountain! Although a part of the range, it stands at the head of the valley, like a monarch taking precedence of a lordly retinue. Two-thirds of its height is above timber-line, bare and desolate, and except for a month or two of midsummer, dazzling white with snow, while in its abysmal gorges it holds eternal reservoirs of ice.

> "Oh, sacred mount with kingly crest
> Through tideless ether reaching,
> The earth-world kneels to hear the prayer
> Thy dusky slopes are teaching.
> With mystic glow on sunset eyes
> All trembling lie thy blood-red leaves,
> Their silken veins with gold inwrought.
> Oh, glorious is thy world-wide thought!"

The lower slopes of the mountain are clad in vast forests of pine and hemlock, while its grand triad of gray granite peaks lift into the sky their sharp pyramidal pinnacles, splintered and furrowed by the storm-compelling and omnipotent hand of the Almighty. To the north and south, for a distance of nearly two hundred miles, it is flanked by the serrated crests of the Sangre de Cristo range, the whole forming a panorama of unexampled grandeur and beauty.

SIERRA BLANCA.

PATIENCE STAPLETON.

North star o'er seas of land,
Mountain, serene and grand,
Sentinel of the Rockies stand,
   Sierra Blanca;
Dial of recorded time
Reared in solitude sublime.

Poets, raptured, long have told
Of the crown of sunset gold
Resting on thy crest so old,
   Sierra Blanca;
In all this land is given
Thee to be nighest Heaven.

Vision to the artist rare
Is the purple robe so fair
Thou with kingly grace doth wear,
   Sierra Blanca;
And thy velvet pall of night,
Crown stars deck with jewels bright.

Once the waves of oceans past—
Silver waves rolling fast—
Sunny spray o'er thee cast,
   Sierra Blanca;
Forests green crept up thy side,
Followed close the ebbing tide.

In the light of that far day
What strange races, who shall say,
Lived their lives and went their way?
   Sierra Blanca;
What strange monsters of the deep
Went to dust in death's last sleep?

Ere that exile on him fell
Once the Indian loved him well,
Happy in thy shades to dwell,
   Sierra Blanca;
Now the wolf in hidden lair
Unmolested scents the air.

Once the Spanish cavalier
Held thee in his heart so dear,
Half in love, half in fear,
   Sierra Blanca;
Martyr priests might happy sigh
At thy glorious feet to die.

Over all the green plains wide
Peace and joy do now abide,
Happy homes below thee hide,
   Sierra Blanca;
High uplifted childish eyes
Liken thee to Paradise.

WAGON WHEEL GAP.

WAGON WHEEL GAP.

ON the Del Norte Branch of the Denver & Rio Grande Railroad is Wagon Wheel Gap, which has become the favorite sporting ground for seekers of health and the lovers of the rod and gun. The scenery is wonderfully beautiful. As the Gap is approached the valley narrows until the river is hemmed in between massive walls of solid rock and rise to such a height on either side as to throw the passage into twilight shadow. The river rushes roaring down over gleaming gravel or precipitous ledges. Progressing, the scene becomes wilder and more romantic, until at last the waters of the Rio Grande pour through a cleft in the rocks just wide enough to allow the construction of a road along the river's edge. On the right, as one enters, tower cliffs to a tremendous height, suggestive in their appearance to the Palisades of the Hudson. On the left rises the round shoulder of a massive mountain. The vast wall is unbroken for more than half a mile, its crest presenting an almost unserrated sky-line. Once through the Gap, the traveler, looking toward the south, sees a valley encroached upon and surrounded by hills

"Bathed in the tenderest purple of distance,
Tinted and shadowed by pencils of air."

Here is an old stage station, a primitive and picturesque structure of hewn logs, made cool and inviting by wide-roofed verandas. Not a hundred feet away rolls the Rio Grande river, swarming with trout. A drive of a mile along a winding road, each turn in which reveals new scenic beauties, brings the tourist to the famous springs. The medicinal qualities of the waters, both of the cold and hot springs, have been thoroughly tested and proved equal, if not superior, to the Hot Springs of Arkansas.

WAGON WHEEL GAP.

BY H. L. WASSON.

So "pretty" expresses the scene to you—
　You only gather what meets the eye,
A charming spot for a picture view;
　A vale where the sunbeams tender lie.

But to us, who know how sublime can be
　This relic of Eden in summer green,
Where the Rio Grande sings of the sea,
　And its silver waves fringe the rocks between,

The word falls null, for our trained ears
　In every ripple detect a sob;
But we face our birthright of toil and tears
　With hearts that beat to a fearless throb.

For have we not seen the Storm King ride
　Through the narrow gorge with his armed Knights,
Their snow-white banners in martial pride
　Defiantly streaming upon the heights;

Have felt the shock as they thundered past,
　On the heart of Nature, pulsing strong,
Their bugle note but a shrieking blast,
　Prolonged and clear as a Norse God's song.

Yes, seen the morning encrown the peaks
　In silver beams on a helmet blue,
And learned the language this grandeur speaks—
　No tempest conquers if faith stands true.

And the scene becomes a cathedral pile—
　A choir in the Rio Grande hymn,
Our passions buried in every aisle,
　And peace, High Priest at the altar dim.

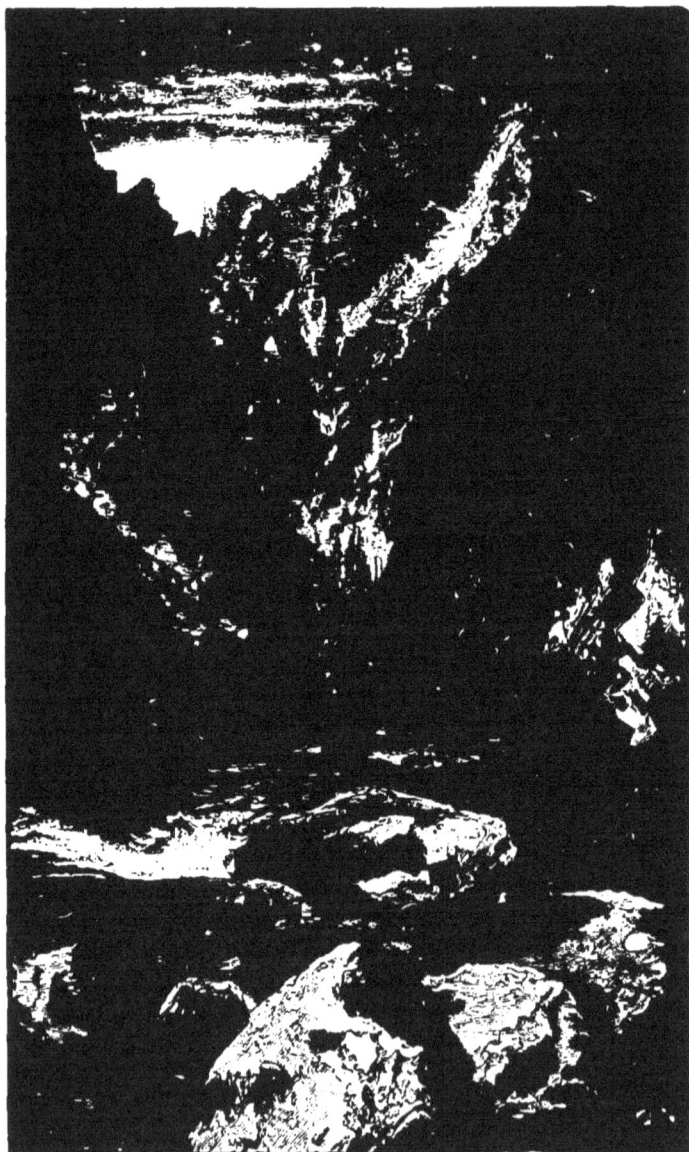

TOLTEC GORGE AND TUNNEL.

TOLTEC GORGE.

AN hour's ride from Antonita brings the traveler to the brow of a precipitous hill, from whence he looks down on the picturesque valley of the Los Pinos. As the advance is made around mountain spurs and deep ravines, glimpses are caught of profound depths and towering heights, and then the train, making a detour of four miles around a side cañon, plunges into the blackness of Toltec tunnel, which is remarkable in that it pierces the summit of the mountain instead of its base. Twelve hundred feet of perpendicular descent would take one to the bottom of the gorge, while the seared and wrinkled expanse of the opposite wall confronts us, lifting its massive bulwarks high above us,

" Fronting heaven's splendor,
Strong and full and clear."

When the train emerges from the tunnel it is upon the brink of a precipice. A solid bridge of trestle-work, set in the rock after the manner of a balcony, supports the track, and from this coigne of vantage the traveler beholds a most thrilling spectacle. The tremendous gorge, whose sides are splintered rocks and monumental crags and whose depths are filled with the snow-white waters of a foaming torrent, lies beneath him, the blue sky is above him and all around the majesty and mystery of the mountains. On the 20th day of September, 1881, the National Association of General Passenger Agents (then on an excursion over the Denver & Rio Grande Railroad), at the time President Garfield was being buried in Cleveland, held memorial services at the mouth of Toltec tunnel and since have erected a beautiful monument in commemoration of the event.

TOLTEC GORGE.

PATIENCE STAPLETON.

Against the snows of cloud hills high,
  Majestic mountains, centuries old,
Reach rugged heights far up the sky,
  Like Babel's tower in story old.

The winds of night in furious rage
  Beat 'gainst the wall 'twixt earth and Heaven;
Each element tireless war did wage;
  Backward, defeated each was driven.

The warm Chinook o'er the prairie sighed;
  The north wind fled to frozen seas;
The chill east wind in coast fogs died;
  The avalanche crashed amid the trees.

Furrowed and tortured, in silent woe,
  One mountain bore the storms of ages,
And sun of summer or winter's snow
  Left no trace on its mystic pages.

But a drift of snow that lay long hidden
  In creviced niche on a lean peak's crest,
Wept bitter tears that crept unchidden
  Far down the mountain's unyielding breast.

The river down in the valley knew,
  For the stream whispered when they met—
The brook and river—and, laughing, too,
  The hills had never a thought as yet.

In years the mountain's heart of rock
  Yields to the subtle brook, and fast,
With thunder peal and earthquake shock,
  Crashed chasm open—defeat at last.

Centuries pass. The deep drifted snows
  Fade 'neath summer suns, and the stream
Widens the gorge, and misty breath throws
  High up black walls that silvery gleam.

But a web is cast of iron strong,
  Like a spider's home of thread-like coil.
The brook is tamed, and its echoing song
  Praises the power of human toil.

ANIMAS CAÑON AND THE NEEDLE MOUNTAINS.

ANIMAS CAÑON.

ANIMAS CAÑON is one of the wildest and most picturesque gorges in the Rocky mountains. Through
it the Rio de las Animas Perdidas, or "River of
Lost Souls," finds its way to the valley below. For a
dozen miles north of Durango the Denver & Rio Grande
Railroad traverses the fertile and cultivated valley of the
Animas in its approach to the cañon. Soon the valley
becomes more broken and contracted, the approaching
walls grow more precipitous and the smooth meadows
give place to stately pines and sighing sycamores. The
silvery Animas frets in its narrowing bed and breaks into
foam against the opposing boulders. The road climbs
and clings to the rising cliffs and presently the earth and
stately pines have receded and the train rolls along a mere
granite shelf in mid-air. Above, the vertical wall rises a
thousand feet; below, hundreds of feet of perpendicular
depth and a fathomless river. The cañon is here a mere
rent in the mountain, so narrow one may toss a pebble
across, and the cramped stream has assumed the deep
emerald hue of the ocean. In the shadows of the rocks
all is solitary, and weird, and awful. The startled traveler
quickly loses all apprehension in the wondrous beauty and
grandeur of the scene and, as successive curves repeat
and enhance the enchantment, nature asserts herself in
ecstacy. Emerging from the marvelous gorge, the bed of
the cañon rapidly rises until the roadway is but a few feet
above the stream. Dark walls of rock are replaced with
clustering mountains of supreme height, whose abruptness
defies the foot of man, and The Needles, the most peculiar
and striking of the Rockies, thrust their splintered pinnacles into the regions of perpetual snow.

RIO DE LAS ANIMAS PERDIDAS.

EDGAR P. VANGASSEN.

Rapid the current rolls
In the river of lost souls!
Rapid and white when the night
Lies swathed in the warm moonlight.
Rapid and white in the day
As it swirls along its way,
Born of the silvery rills
In the pine and cedared hills.
  Flashing, dashing,
  Swirling, crashing,
Moaning in the gulch of shadow,
Laughing through the shining meadow,
Hugging close the rocky rifts,
Gliding amid boulder drifts;
  Loving, smiling,
  Care beguiling,
Cool and limpid in the shade;
Warm and sunny in the glade;
Rapid the current rolls
In the river of lost souls.

   *   *   *   *

Still I linger by the stream
As if in a pleasant dream,
With the current running down
Through the cañon, past the town,
To the pleasant lands that lie
Underneath a southern sky.
Let the snow rest on the hills,
Let the snow melt in the rills,
So the shining volume flows
Where the peach's pink bloom blows.

Lotos land in legend lies
Hidden amid shadowed skies;
Here, a human Eden waits
At the shining river's gates,
Opening for willing hands
Into fruitful orchard lands.
Souls lost in such vale as this
Wake again in lands of bliss.
He who in these meadows stands
Holds Love's Lotos in his hands.

HOMES OF THE CLIFF DWELLERS.

HOMES OF THE CLIFF-DWELLERS.

ONE of the most attractive portions of Colorado, to the scientist, antiquarian and, indeed, the general tourist, is that part in which are found the cliff-dwellings of a long extinct race. A brief description of one found in Mancos cañon will serve as a characterization of all. Perched seven hundred feet above the valley, on a little ledge only just large enough to hold it, stands a two-story house made of finely-cut sandstone, each block about fourteen by six inches, accurately fitted and set in mortar, now harder than the stone itself. The floor is the ledge of rock and the roof the overhanging cliff. There are three rooms on the ground floor, each one six by nine feet, with partition walls of faced stone. Traces of a floor which once separated the upper from the lower story still remain. Each of the stories is six feet in height and all the rooms are nicely plastered and painted what now looks a dull brick red color, with a white band along the floor. The windows are square apertures with no signs of glazing, commanding a view of the whole valley for many miles. The illustration shows a fortified watch-tower, indicating that these strange cliff-dwelling people were prepared to resist assault. Traditions are few and of history there is nothing concerning this lost race. Their ruined houses only remain and some broken fragments of the implements made use of in war and peace. Typical cliff-dwellings are found near Espanola, the southern terminus of the New Mexico extension of the Denver & Rio Grande Railroad, and in the Animas valley, twenty-five miles south of Durango. Researches are in progress concerning these extremely interesting ruins and new facts are being developed concerning their architecture, but it is quite improbable that any certain light will ever be thrown on their origin or history.

HOMES OF THE CLIFF-DWELLERS.

HEADLANDS OF HOVEN-WEEP.

STANLEY WOOD.

In the sad Southwest, in the mystical Sunland,
   Far from the toil and the turmoil of gain;
Hid in the heart of the only—the one land
   Beloved of the Sun, and bereft of the rain;
The one weird land where the wild winds blowing,
   Sweep with a wail o'er the plains of the dead,
A ruin, ancient beyond all knowing,
   Rears its head.

On the cañon's side, in the ample hollow,
   That the keen winds carved in ages past,
The Castle walls, like the nest of a swallow,
   Have clung and have crumbled to this at last.
The ages since man's foot has rested
   Within these walls, no man may know;
For here the fierce grey eagle nested
   Long ago.

Above those walls the crags lean over,
   Below, they dip to the river's bed;
Between, fierce-wingèd creatures hover,
   Beyond, the plain's wild waste is spread.
No foot has climbed the pathway dizzy,
   That crawls away from the blasted heath,
Since last it felt the ever busy
   Foot of Death.

In that haunted castle—it must be haunted,
   For men have lived here, and men have died,
And maidens loved, and lovers daunted,
   Have hoped and feared, have laughed and sighed—
In that haunted Castle the dust has drifted,
   But the eagles only may hope to see
What shattered Shrines and what Altars rifted,
   There may be.

The white, bright rays of the sunbeam sought it,
  The cold, clear light of the moon fell here,
The west wind sighed, and the south wind brought it,
  Songs of Summer year after year.
Runes of Summer, but mute and runeless,
  The Castle stood; no voice was heard,
Save the harsh, discordant, wild and tuneless
  Cry of bird.

The spring rains poured, and the torrent rifted
  A deeper way;—the foam-flakes fell,
Held for a moment poised and lifted,
  Down to a fiercer whirlpool's hell.
On the Castle tower no guard, in wonder,
  Paused in his marching to and fro,
For on the turret the mighty thunder
  Found no foe.

No voice of Spring—no Summer glories
  May wake the warders from their sleep,
Their graves are made by the sad Dolores,
  And the barren headlands of Hoven-weep.
Their graves are nameless—their race forgotten,
  Their deeds, their words, their fate, are one
With the mist, long ages past begotten,
  Of the Sun.

Those castled cliffs they made their dwelling,
  They lived and loved, they fought and fell,
No faint, far voice comes to us telling
  More than those crumbling walls can tell.
They lived their life, their fate fulfilling,
  Then drew their last faint, faltering breath,
Their hearts, congealed, clutched by the chilling
  Hand of Death.

Dismantled towers, and turrets broken,
  Like grim and war-worn braves who keep
A silent guard, with grief unspoken
  Watch o'er the graves by the Hoven-weep.
The nameless graves of a race forgotten;
  Whose deeds, whose words, whose fate are one
With the mist, long ages past begotten,
  Of the Sun.

THE ROYAL GORGE

THE ROYAL GORGE.

THE crowning wonder of this wonderful Denver &
Rio Grande Railroad is the Royal Gorge. Situated
between Cañon City and Salida, it is easy of access
either from Denver or Pueblo. After the entrance of the
cañon has been made, surprise and almost terror comes.
The train rolls around a long curve close under a wall
of black and banded granite, beside which the ponderous
locomotive shrinks to a mere dot, as if swinging on
some pivot in the heart of the mountain, or captured
by a centripetal force that would never resign its grasp.
Almost a whole circle is accomplished and the grand
amphitheatrical sweep of the wall shows no break in its
smooth and zenith-cutting façade. Will the journey end
here? Is it a mistake that this crevice goes through the
range? Does not all this mad water gush from some
powerful spring, or boil out of a subterranean channel
impenetrable to us? No, it opens. Resisting centripetal,
centrifugal force claims the train and it breaks away at a
tangent past the edge or round the corner of the great
black wall which compelled its detour and that of the
river before it. Now, what glories of rock-piling confront
the wide distended eye. How those sharp-edged cliffs,
standing with upright heads that play at hand-ball with
the clouds, alternate with one another, so that first the
right, then the left, then the right one beyond strike our
view, each one half obscured by its fellow in front, each
showing itself level-browed with its comrades as we come
even with it, each a score of hundreds of dizzy feet in
height, rising perpendicular from the water and the track,
splintered atop into airy pinnacles, braced behind against
the almost continental mass through which the chasm has
been cleft. This is the Royal Gorge !

THE ROYAL GORGE.

G. G. FERGUSON.

In the Royal Gorge I stand,
  With its mountain forms around me,
With infinity behind me and infinity before;
  Cliff and chasm on every hand,
Peaks and pinnacles surround me;
  At my feet the river rushes with its never-ceasing roar.

*   *   *   *   *   *   *   *

Oh! the power that piled these wonders,
  As the mountains took their stations;
As a great red belt rose upward in a glittering zone of fire.
  Oh! the crash of blended thunders
Shaking earth to its foundations,
  As each struggling cliff rose upward, climbing higher, ever higher.

Oh! the crashing and the groaning,
  And the deep and awful shudder
As that great red belt was parted and the mountains crashed in twain;
  And the Arkansas came roaring,
Raging with its dreadful thunder,
  Sweeping through the mighty chasm dashing madly toward the main.

Oh! this myriad crested cañon,
  With its walls of massive marble,
With the granite and red sandstone piled in peaks that pierce the sky;
  Where no bird dare dip its pinion
In the narrow veil of azure,
  Where the solemn shadows linger o'er the river rolling by.

Mortal! ere you enter here,
  Pause and bare thy brow before Him,
You are entering a temple which the Mighty One did rear.
  Put thy shoes from off thy feet,
And with sacred awe adore Him,
  Throned in awful might and majesty, the Great One dwelleth here.

UPPER TWIN LAKE.

TWIN LAKES.

THE TWIN LAKES possess peculiar merits as a place of resort. Lying at an altitude of 9,357 feet at the mouth of a cañon, in a little nook, surrounded by lofty mountains, from whose never-failing snows their waters are fed, their seclusions invite the tired denizens of dusty cities to fly from debilitating heat and the turmoil of traffic to a quiet haven where "Jack Frost" makes himself at home in July and August. The lakes are easily reached by an hour's ride from Granite, a station on the Leadville Branch of the Denver & Rio Grande Railroad. On the lakes are numerous sail and row-boats and fishing tackle can always be obtained. Both lakes are well stocked with fish and the neighboring streams also abound in mountain trout. The scene is of surpassing beauty and one is loth to leave

"The green sea wave, whose waters gleam
Limpid, as if her mines of pearl
Were melted all to form the stream;
And her fair islets, small and bright,
With their green shores reflected there,
Look like those Peri isles of light
That hang by spell-work in the air."

Surrounding the lakes are large forests of pine which add their characteristic odor to the air. The nearest mountains, whose forms are reflected in the placid waters, are Mount Elbert, 14,351 feet in height, La Plata, 14,311 (each higher than Pike's Peak), Lake mountain and the Twin Peaks. Just across the narrow Arkansas valley rises Mount Sheridan, far above timber line, flanked by the hoary summits of Park range. Twin Lakes is one of the highest of the popular Rocky mountain resorts and furnishes an unfailing "antidote" for hot weather.

TWIN LAKES.

THE YACHT DAUNTLESS.

HELEN HUNT JACKSON IN YOUTHS COMPANION.

Far off in the Rocky mountains
    And two miles up in the air,
Lie the Twin Lakes, close together,
    All rippling, shining and fair.

The mountains wall in the water;
    It looks like a great blue cup;
And the sky looks like another
    Turned over, bottom side up.

'Tis the sweetest place I know of;
    No sweeter one could be planned
For summer and winter pleasure
    On the water and the land.

Each sunset and sunrise, glowing
    With bright colors, spread the lake,
And along the shore gay blossoms
    Even brighter colors make.

But there were only little row-boats
    Which crept o'er the water blue,
And every one said, " If only
    With a swelling sail we flew! "

" We'll fly with a sail all swelling,
    And make light work of the miles!
I'll build with my hands a vessel,"
    Cried out the good Captain Stiles.

So he hewed him down great fir-trees,
    And hewed him logs of the pine,
And the splendid slender balsams,
    All full of fragrances fine.

And he sawed and planed and hammered
    With tools of good iron and steel,
And he made the deck all shining,
    And bent and hollowed the keel.

And he set the mast of balsam
    Upright, as it used to grow,
And he sewed a sail of canvas,
    And a pennon white as snow.

And I wonder when he launched it
    What the birds thought overhead—
If they thought it was another
    Great bird with its wings outspread.

Then he christened it " The Dauntless,"
    Though why I could never see;
· For a ship more free from danger
    In the world there could not be.

So long as she holds together,
    With her timbers strong and sound,
The lake will but gently rock her,
    The mountains will wall her round.

Far off in the Rocky mountains,
    And two miles up in the air,
On the lake so blue and shining,
    Her light burdens she will bear.

And if you will come some summer
    And journey our mountains through,
You can sail in this Yacht Dauntless,
    And see I have told you true!

MOUNT OF THE HOLY CROSS.

MOUNT OF THE HOLY CROSS.

FROM the crest of Fremont Pass, and also from Tennessee Pass, can be seen the Mount of the Holy Cross. It is a summit that would attract the eye anywhere, its foot hidden in verdurous hills, guarded by knightly crags half buried in seething clouds, its helmet vertical, frowning, plumed with gleaming snow,

"Aye, every inch a king."

The snow-white emblem of the Christian faith gleams with bright splendor against an azure sky. The cross is formed by two transverse cañons of immense depth riven down and across the summit of the mountain. In these cañons lies eternal snow. The symbol is perfect in shape, and while gazing with wonder and awe upon this "sign set in the heavens," th adventurous wayfarer at last realizes that he has reached that height "around whose summit splendid visions rise" and those thrilling lines of Keats come involuntarily to his lips:

"Then felt I like some watcher of the skies
When a new planet swims into his ken;
Or like stout Cortes, when with eagle eyes
He stared at the Pacific—and all his men
Looked at each other with a wild surmise—
Silent upon a peak in Darien."

Shining grandly out of the pure ether and above all turbulence of earthly strife, it seems to say: "Humble thyself, O man! Uncover thy head, forget not that as high as gleams the splendor of this ever-living cross above thy gilded spires, so are the thoughts of its Creator above thy thoughts, his ways above thy ways."

MOUNT OF THE HOLY CROSS.

WILL L. VISCHER.

Where Nature's God hath roughest wrought;
    Where spring the purest fountains;
Where long ago the Titans fought
    And hurled for missiles, mountains;
Where everlasting snows abide,
    And tempest clouds are driven
Along the solid granite side
    Of yawning cañons, riven
Deep in the Rockies' grandest pride
    That lifts its head to heaven;

Amid the wilds, where awful rise
    The giant peaks, that fathom
Night's starry depths and day's blue skies,
    And brood above the chasm,
One monarch 'mongst the mighty hills
    Rears high his summit hoary,
Like some grim king whose legend fills
    A page of olden story,
And heart o'erawes and soul enthrills
    Before his regal glory.

The holy cross of Christian faith,
Above the royal velvet
    In beauty shines, an emblem wraith,
High on the beetling helmet;
    Its white arms stretching through the sheen
Of silvery mist, are gleaming;
    A talisman, the world to screen,
Hope's symbol, in its seeming;
    A wonder grand, a joy serene,
Upon the ages beaming.

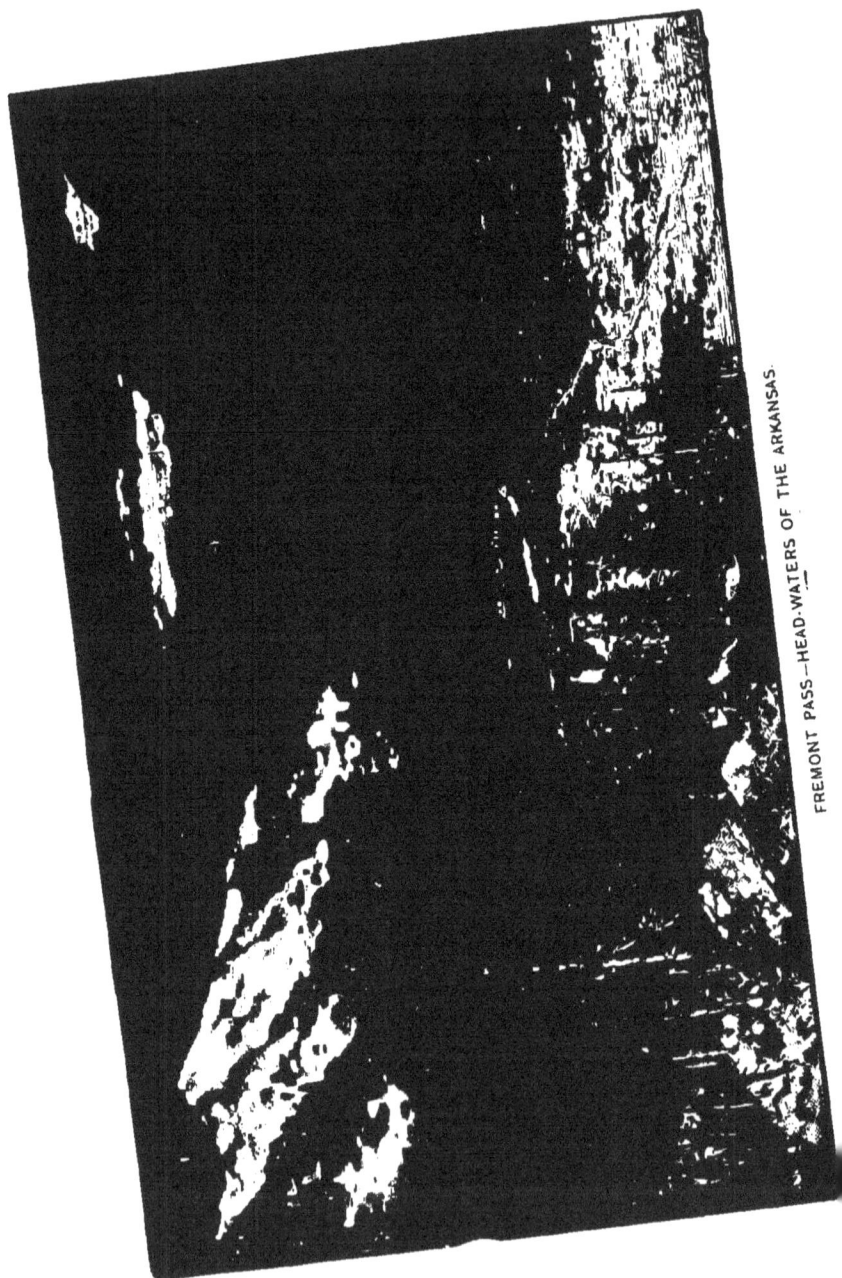

FREMONT PASS—HEAD-WATERS OF THE ARKANSAS.

FREMONT PASS.

THROUGH an Arcadian valley the approach to Fremont Pass is made. A famous pass with the historic name of him who has been called the "pathfinder," although a later day has witnessed greater achievements than his among the Rocky mountains. A journey here deserves the name of a pilgrimage, for from the summit of the Pass the traveler can discern the "Mount of the Holy Cross." The ascent is one replete with vivid interest. Fainter and fainter grow the lines of objects in the valley, until at last the clouds envelop the train, and at the next moment the traveler looks down upon a rolling mass of vapor through which the light strikes in many colored beams. The sublimity of the scene forbids all thoughts other than those of reverence and rapture. The Denver & Rio Grande Railroad crosses the pass at an altitude of eleven thousand five hundred and forty feet, higher than any iron trail yet established in North America or the Old World. Down in the valley the Arkansas river has its source in a little rivulet one could stand astride like another Colossus of Rhodes.

> "There in the gorges that widen, descending
> From cloud and from cold into summer eternal,
> Gather the threads of the ice-gendered fountains—
> Gather to riotous torrents of crystal,
> And giving each shelvy recess where they dally
> The blooms of the north and its evergreen turfage."

This little brook pushes its way eastward, escapes through the Grand cañon with indescribable turmoil, and always growing bigger, broader and stronger, deeper and more dignified until it leaves the mountains, finally strikes boldly across a thousand miles of rolling prairie to join the mighty Mississippi on its way to the sea.

FREMONT PASS.

J. D. DILLENBACK.

He who has climbed in this rare atmosphere,
By giddy roads, up to this lofty height
And paused upon the pass, awed by the sight,
Looks forth in wonder, shadowed still by fear.

The snow-crowned monarchs of an upper world,
Rugged and steep and bare, the mountains rise;
Their very feet are planted in the skies;
Adown their sides are avalanches hurled.

Man seldom, for adventure or for gain,
To greater heights ascends. Here is the crest
Of the great Rocky Mountains; East and West
Drop toward the Atlantic and Pacific main.

Time was, when few and daring were the men
Who might behold this pass, that Fremont gained
Through toil and danger, and, its heights attained,
Perils beset the long leagues down again.

Now all may come who seek, afar from crowds,
The grand in nature, for we now engage
The potent genii of this iron age,
Fire, steam and steel, and rise above the clouds!

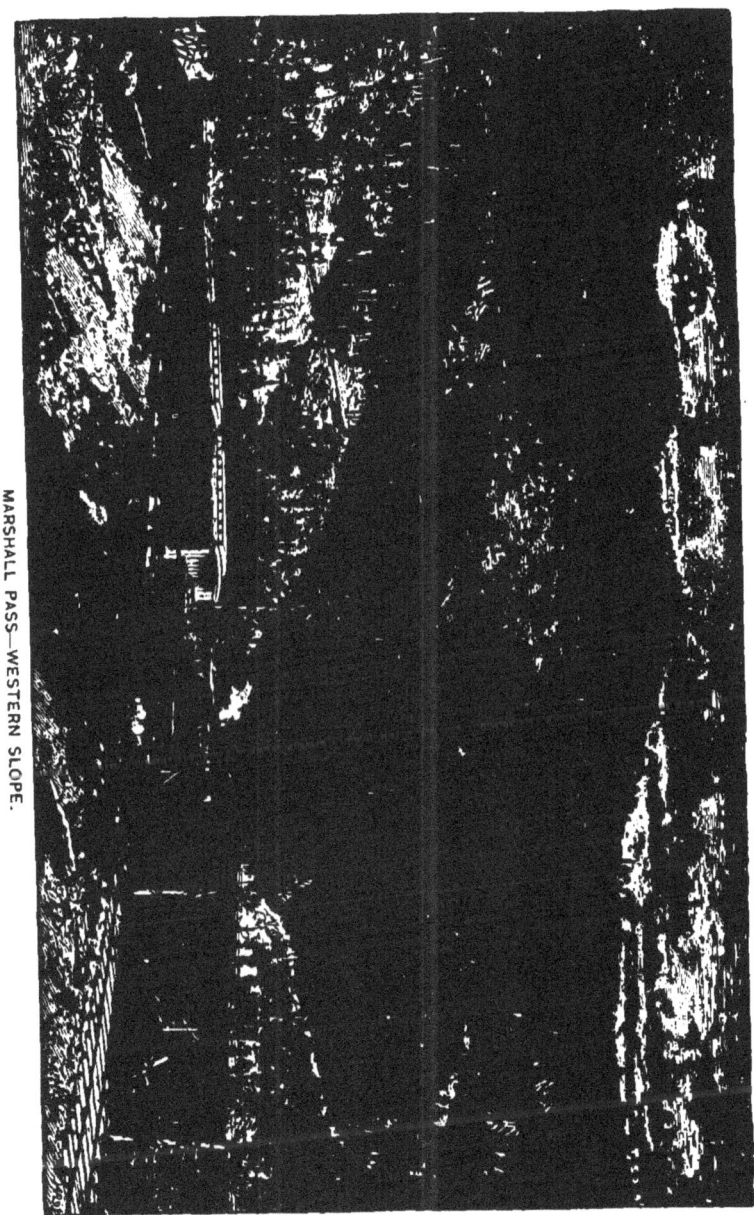

MARSHALL PASS—WESTERN SLOPE.

MARSHALL PASS.

MARSHALL PASS is entered almost imperceptibly from Poncha Pass and the whole wonderful ascent might very readily be imagined as one and the same. The summit is almost eleven thousand feet above the sea and the tortuous method by which the daring engineers of the Denver & Rio Grande Railroad have achieved this summit can best be understood by a glance at the cut illustrating the alignment of the track shown on another page. As the train progresses up the steep, the view becomes less obstructed by mountain sides and the eye roams over miles of cone-shaped summits. The timberless tops of towering ranges show him that he is among the heights and in a region familiar with the clouds. Then he beholds, stretching away to the left, the most perfect of all, the Sierras. The sunlight falls with a white, transfiguring radiance upon the snow-crowned spires of the Sangre de Christo range. Their sharp and dazzling pyramids, which near at hand are clearly defined, extend to the southward until cloud and sky and snowy peak commingle and form a vague and bewildering vision. To the right towers the fire-scarred front of old Ouray, grand, solitary and forbidding. Ouray holds the pass, standing sentinel at the rocky gateway to the fertile Gunnison. Slowly the steeps are conquered, until at last the train halts upon the summit of the continental divide which separates the waters of the Atlantic and Pacific. The traveler looks down upon four lines of road, terrace beyond terrace, the last so far below as to be quite indistinct to view. Wonder at the triumphs of engineering skill is strangely mingled with the feelings of awe and admiration at the stupendous grandeur of the scene.

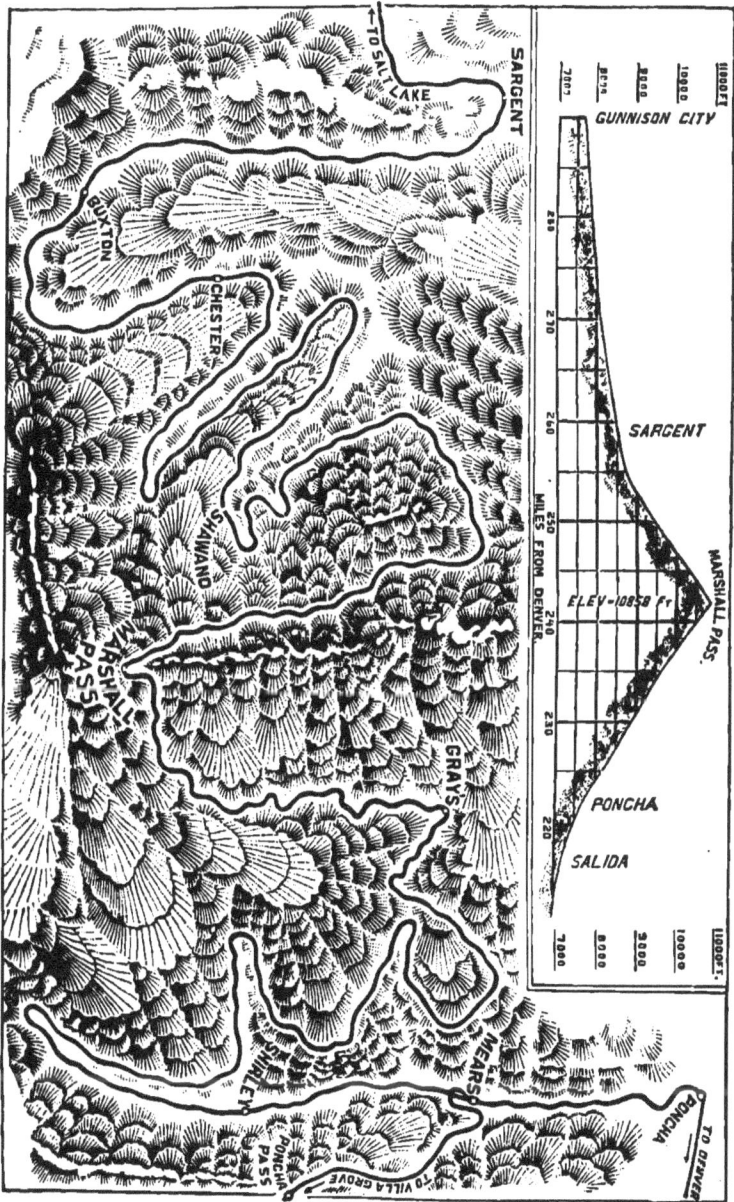

ALIGNMENT OF THE D. & R. G. R. R. OVER MARSHALL PASS

MARSHALL PASS.

ALICE S. MITCHELL.

Above the world's wild roar and clash
Unnumbered waves of emerald dash,
One giant rears a lofty dome,
His wrinkled forehead flecked with foam.
Here smoky pennons wave in air,
Two armies grand, the brave, the fair
Wind swiftly up the mountain side.
They reach the cleft, the great "divide;
With joyful shout, upon its crest,
The East gives greeting to the West.
Here generations yet unborn
Shall watch the sunset kiss the morn,
And glad winds "hallelujahs" sing
As Winter clasps the hand of Spring.

Upon the summit of this crest
Columbia's eagle built his nest.
The plumage of his mighty wings
From sea to sea their shadow flings.
Sheltered beneath this faithful breast
A continent doth safely rest.
Guarded by piercing eyes so true
His beek holds firm the banner blue.

Sometimes to mortal man 'tis given
To breathe the perfumed air of heaven,
The folded wings of souls unfurled
Like soaring birds above the world,
Mounting beyond our love and hate
We, reverent, whisper "God is great."

CHIPPETA FALLS IN THE BLACK CAÑON.

THE BLACK CAÑON.

IN all the world there is no place so beautiful, imposing,
sublime and awful that may be so easily and comfort-
ably visited as the Black cañon, for the iron horse of
the Denver & Rio Grande Railroad has a pathway through
the cañon and he draws after him coaches as handsome
and pleasant as those which he draws on the level plain.
Along many miles of this grand gorge the railway lies
upon a shelf that has been blasted in the solid walls of
God's. masonry; walls that stand sheer two thousand feet
in height and so close together that for most of the distance through the cañon only a streak of sky, sometimes
in broad daylight, spangled with stars, is seen above.

> " I'll look no more ;
> Lest my brain turn, and the deficient sight
> Topple down headlong."

Unlike many of the Colorado cañons, the scenery in this
one is kaleidoscopic, ever changing. Here the train glides
along between the close, regular and exalted walls, then
suddenly it passes the mouth of another mighty cañon
which looks as.if it were a great gateway to an unroofed
arcade leading from the pathway of some monstrous
giant. Now, at a sharp turn, Chippeta falls, a stream of
liquid crystal, pitches from the top of the dizzy cliffs to
the bosom of the sparkling river which dashes beside the
road. Then a spacious amphitheater is passed, in the
center of which stands Currecanti Needle solitary and
alone, a towering monument of solid stone, which reaches
to where it flaunts the clouds, like some great cathedral
spire. Truly there is no gorge in all the Rocky range
that presents such variety and grandeur as the Black
cañon of the Gunnison.

CURRECANTI NEEDLE—BLACK CAÑON

THE BLACK CAÑON.

FANNIE ISABEL SHERRICK.

The midday sun in this deep gorge
 Resigns his old-time splendor,
His palace walls of dreamy gold
 The rose-hues warm and tender.
 The cleft is dark below
Where foaming flows the somber river,
The wild winds sigh and blossoms shiver.
And violet mists ascending
 Obscure the Orient glow.

O! rushing river emerald-hued,
 How mad thou art and fearless,
No frowning gates, though granite-barred,
 Can curb thy waters peerless!
 The silent gods of stone
Revoke their ancient laws of might
When through the gorge with wing-swift flight
Thy wind-tossed waves are speeding,
 Each moment wilder grown.

The faint stars shine in broad midday
 Through twilight mists, gold-rifted,
Where opal streams make dizzy leaps
 O'er jasper walls blue-rifted.
 Below no naiads dream
'Neath dim arcades, through sunless deeps
The nomad river lonely leaps,
Where castled crags rise skyward
 Like watch-towers o'er the stream.

On massive cliff-walls Nature's hand
 Has turned time's sun-worn pages,
In faces carved and figures hewn
 We trace the work of ages.
 The gold-tipped spires sublime,
That pierce the sky-like shafts of light,
But mark the measureless heavenward height
Of Nature's own cathedral,
 Whose stern high priest is Time.

In this grand temple, eons old
 Her organ notes are pealing,
In gold-flecked arch and wave-worn aisles
 The flower-nuns are kneeling;
 Her altars echo prayer,
And when at dusk the cold moon shines,
O! awful are the far white shrines
From earth to God upreaching
 Through spirit-flooded air.

CASTLE GATE.

CASTLE GATE.

GUARDING the entrance to Price River cañon, through which the railroad runs into the very heart of the range, stands Castle Gate, similar in many respects to the gateway of the Garden of the Gods. The two huge pillars or ledges of rock composing it are offshoots of the cliffs behind. They are of different heights, one measuring five hundred and the other four hundred and fifty feet from top to base. They are richly dyed with red and the firs and pines growing about them, but reaching only to their lower strata, render this coloring more noticeable and beautiful. Between the two sharp promontories, which are separated only by a narrow space, the river and the railroad both run, one pressing closely against the other. The stream leaps over a rocky bed and its banks are lined with tangled brush. The turreted rocks, the rushing stream and the darkling cañon bring forcibly to mind that wonderful dream of Coleridge:

> "In Xanadu did Kubla Khan
> A stately pleasure-dome decree;
> Where Alph, the sacred river, ran
> Through caverns measureless to man,
>   Down to a sunless sea.
> So twice five miles of fertile ground
>   With walls and towers were girdled round;
> And here were gardens bright with sinuous rills,
>   Where blossom'd many an incense-bearing tree;
> And here were forests ancient as the hills,
>   Infolding sunny spots of greenery."

Once past the gate, and looking back, the bold headlands forming it have a new and more attractive beauty. They are higher and more massive, it seems, than when we were in their shadow. Huge rocks project far out from their perpendicular faces. No other isolated pinnacles in this region approach them in size or majesty. They are landmarks up and down the cañon, their lofty tops catching the eye before their bases are discovered.

AT CASTLE GATE.

W. E. PABOR.

"Stand, stranger, stand. The castle gate
    Through which you pass to fairy land
Is mine to guard. What happy fate
    Bids you within its border? Stand!"

Warder of this stately castle,
    Stay the menace of your hand,
I am but a simple singer
    Singing songs throughout the land.
Through the time-stained rugged portals
    I can catch a glimpse afar,
Where the light shines on the woodland
    Like the light of the morning star.

Let me pass, Oh stern-faced warder,
    Through the wondrous castle gate;
Let me walk within the garden
    Led by fancy and by fate.
For the sunlight and the moonlight
    And the starlight, as they fall,
Seem replete with happy fancies
    Making pictures on the wall.

Gateway to a happy valley,
    Open wide and let my feet
Wander in the flowery meadows
    Where the shining waters meet.
Frowning cliffs lift up to front me,
    Sunset hues the rocks that rise,
But my eyes have caught a vision
    Of green fields and violet skies.

Lying over Soldier Summit
    In the valleys of the West,
With the bloom and blush of Eden
    Lying softly on their breast,
Vales of splendor, vales of beauty,
    Meet to melt a heart of stone;
Vale of Tempe pales in glory
    When beside thy brightness shown.

Other lips have uttered fancies,
    Other eyes on thee have shone,
Other feet have walked these meadows,
    Passing through the gate of stone.
But my lips can not keep silence,
    Or my eyes their rapture bate,
As they catch a glimpse of Eden
    Through the cliff-crowned Castle Gate.

"Pass, stranger, pass, the olden time
    Was full of song of mirth and cheer;
Sing any song that suits your rhyme,
    And let it echo round the year."

SALT LAKE CITY—TEMPLE AND TABERNACLE.

GREAT SALT LAKE.

SALT LAKE CITY is in a veritable garden. Low and picturesque houses harmonize in their cool, quiet tones with the extensive orchards of fruit and gardens of flowers which surround them and the business blocks in the center of the city are imposing and strong. Back upon a "bench," and several hundred feet above the city, is Fort Douglas, the flag of the Republic standing out in bright relief against the Wasatch. Strong and rapid mountain streams come rushing through the cañons and are led into the city, where the clear, cold, limpid waters sing a pleasant song as they sport and play along the sides of the streets where they are conducted through the entire city. The Oquirrh mountains shut in the valley to the west. The great object of interest to the tourist and stranger is Temple Square; here are situated the great ecclesiastical buildings of the Mormon Church. Prominent among them is the Temple, Tabernacle and Assembly Hall.

The Great Salt Lake is a mysterious inland sea, which, more than any other body of water on the globe, has created and left unsatisfied the curiosity of mankind. Its dead, dreamy, silent, tideless waters are still an enigma, both to the learned and unlearned. Here one can recall with aptness Byron's apostrophe to Leman:

"Lake Leman woos me with its crystal face,
  The mirror where the stars and mountains view
The stillness of their aspect in each trace
  Its clear depth yields of their far height and hue."

The lake's surface is higher than the Alleghanies and mountainous islands rise from its bosom, casting their dark shadows on the blue expanse which lies slumbering at their feet.

THE GREAT SALT LAKE.

SUNSET ON GREAT SALT LAKE.

W. E. PABOR.

Over the Oquirrh ranges
  Pearly clouds of softness rest,
Blending with the rippling changes
  On great Salt Lake's wave-swept breast.
In the sunset I am roaming,
  Looking out across the deep
Tideless waves, that in the gloaming
  Moan as if in dreamy sleep.

Locked in the embrace of mountains,
  Whose green frontlets watch the isles,
Guarding the enchanted fountains
  Where a siren sits and smiles.
Lake of mystery and wonder,
  Lake of silence so sublime,
In thy depths we look and ponder
  On the strangest gift of time.

Lower down the crimson chamber
  Of the west the sunset falls;
Creamy cumuli of amber
  Penciled on its crystal walls;
Now the tints change into umber,
  Twilight shadows creep along
Slowly, like the sense of slumber,
  Through the solace of a song.

As the sunset's charm thrills through me,
  Musing on the sand-swept marge,
Fancy brings a boatman to me
  With his pearl-enameled barge;
And he bids me leave the highlands,
  With their shadow and their stain,
And sail with him to the islands
  Lying in the azure main.

Farewell now to all things human,
  In the boatman's barge I stand,
Trust of man or love of woman
  I leave on the shore of sand.
Through empurpled mists that hover
  Round the islands of the blest,
In the sunset I go over
  To the lotus land of rest.

L'ENVOY.

Through wond'rous scenes our pleasant path has wound
From "Palmer Lake" to that enchanted ground
The "Garden of the Gods." We've paused to view
The many marvels of fair "Manitou."
Have gazed with reverence upon "Cheyenne,"
Made doubly sacred by the poet's pen
And poet's grave; have seen the mighty earth
Grow small beneath us, and new stars take birth
As "Veta Pass" was conquered, and with brown
Rocks girded, gazed on "Blanca's" triple crown;
Have passed o'er "Toltec," marvelous, sublime!
Triumphant work of science, art and time;
Have seen the "Castles" of that perished race
Who dwelt on cliffs, and have beheld the place,
Wondrous and wild, where flows the "Animas"
Through cloven cliffs which let its waters pass.
Then northward turned we've seen upreared on high
The "Holy Cross" emblazoned on the sky,
From "Fremont Pass" beheld beneath our feet
The soaring eagle ply his pinions fleet.
Deep in the "Royal Gorge" have breathless whirled
As through some cavern of the under-world.
On "Marshall Pass" the clouds have by us sped
Like white-sailed ships with all their canvas spread,
Then circling downward to the verdant plain,
Through which the Gunnison flows to the main,
We reach the cañon "Black" and deep and long
Wherein the river sings its battle song;
We pass beyond to where the warders wait
Beside the portals of the "Castle Gate."
Through this we pass to that enchanted sea
The "Great Salt Lake," enwrapped in mystery,
And as it slumbers 'neath the setting sun,
We sigh to think our wondrous journey's done.

www.ingramcontent.com/pod-product-compliance
Lightning Source LLC
Chambersburg PA
CBHW021536270326
41930CB00008B/1280